# Dear Parent:
## Your child's love of reading starts here!

Every child learns to read in a different way and at his or her own speed. Some go back and forth between reading levels and read favorite books again and again. Others read through each level in order. You can help your young reader improve and become more confident by encouraging his or her own interests and abilities. From books your child reads with you to the first books he or she reads alone, there are I Can Read Books for every stage of reading:

### SHARED READING
Basic language, word repetition, and whimsical illustrations, ideal for sharing with your emergent reader

### BEGINNING READING
Short sentences, familiar words, and simple concepts for children eager to read on their own

### READING WITH HELP
Engaging stories, longer sentences, and language play for developing readers

### READING ALONE
Complex plots, challenging vocabulary, and high-interest topics for the independent reader

### ADVANCED READING
Short paragraphs, chapters, and exciting themes for the perfect bridge to chapter books

**I Can Read Books** have introduced children to the joy of reading since 1957. Featuring award-winning authors and illustrators and a fabulous cast of beloved characters, I Can Read Books set the standard for beginning readers.

A lifetime of discovery begins with the magical words **"I Can Read!"**

*Visi* *tion*
*on en* *rience.*

D0035813

To Lori Collins, Editor-in-Chief of Early Childhood
Publications at the National Wildlife Federation.
—J.B.

The author would like to thank David Mizejewski, the naturalist at the
National Wildlife Federation, for his guidance and expertise.

The National Wildlife Federation and Ranger Rick contributors: Children's
Publication and Licensing Staff.

I Can Read Book® is a trademark of HarperCollins Publishers.

Ranger Rick: I Wish I Was a Gorilla
The National Wildlife Federation
Copyright © 2018. All rights reserved.
Manufactured in China. No part of this book may be used or reproduced in any manner whatsoever without
written permission except in the case of brief quotations embodied in critical articles and reviews. For
information address HarperCollins Children's Books, a division of HarperCollins Publishers, 195 Broadway,
New York, NY 10007.
www.icanread.com
www.RangerRick.com

ISBN 978-0-06-243211-7 (trade bdg.)—ISBN 978-0-06-243210-0 (pbk.)

Typography by Brenda E. Angelilli

17 18 19 20 21   SCP   10 9 8 7 6 5 4 3 2 1   ❖   First Edition

RANGER RICK
NATIONAL WILDLIFE FEDERATION

# Ranger Rick

## I Wish I Was a Gorilla

by Jennifer Bové

HARPER

*An Imprint of HarperCollinsPublishers*

What if you wished you were a gorilla?

Then you became a young gorilla.

Could you eat like a gorilla?

Sleep like a gorilla?

Live in a gorilla family?

And would you want to? Find out!

## Where would you live?

Gorillas live in African rainforests.
Many trees and plants grow there.
Rainforests stay green all year.
The weather is often cloudy
with lots of rainy days.

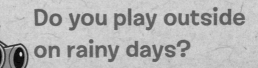

Do you play outside
on rainy days?

## What would your family be like?

A gorilla family is called a troop. The troop has one father gorilla. He is called a silverback because of the light-colored fur that grows on his back.

He leads the troop as they move around the forest.
He finds good things to eat and cozy places to sleep at night.

There are many mother gorillas
that live in a troop.
A mother gorilla feeds milk
to her baby.
She cuddles and kisses her baby.
A baby gorilla rides on its mom's back
wherever she goes.

Gorillas watch their babies closely
to keep them safe.

When a dangerous animal comes near,

a mother gorilla picks up

her baby and runs.

A father gorilla chases

the animal away.

**How would you learn to be a gorilla?**

As baby gorillas grow bigger,

they begin to play a lot.

Playing helps young gorillas learn

to move like grown-up gorillas.

They run around and climb trees.

What games do you play with friends?

Gorillas play with friends, too.

They wrestle and chase one another.

Playing games teaches them

how to get along with other gorillas.

## How would you talk?

Gorillas grunt to say "I'm happy."

They chuckle to say "That's funny."

A hoot says, "I'm excited!"

A bark or scream says, "I'm scared!"

A silverback smacks his chest loudly
to say, "Stay away from my troop!"

What would you
say in gorilla?

**What would you eat?**

Gorillas eat plants.

They like leaves and stems.

They also eat roots and fruits.

Sometimes they eat insects, too.

Older gorillas show young ones which plants are good to eat.

If you ate like a gorilla, what food would you miss?

**How would you wash up?**

Gorillas help one another stay clean.

This is called grooming.

They pick dirt and bugs off friends.
They use their fingers and teeth
to comb one another's hair.

## Where would you sleep?

Young gorillas sleep in tree nests made of leaves and branches. Sometimes their mothers join them. Silverbacks sleep in ground nests. The troop goes to sleep at sunset and wakes up at sunrise.

Would you like to grow up that fast?

## How would growing up change you?

Young gorillas grow up pretty fast.

By the time they are four years old,

they find their own food

and build their own nests.

They leave their troop by age ten

and form new troops of their own.

Being a gorilla could be cool

for a while.

But do you want to talk with grunts?

Sleep in a nest?

Or eat plants and bugs?

Luckily, you don't have to.

You're not a gorilla.

You're YOU!

# Did You Know?

🐾 Gorillas are the world's largest primates.

🐾 Gorillas can live for thirty-five years in the wild.

🐾 A silverback gorilla can eat forty pounds of plants in one day.

🐾 A gorilla's arms are longer than its legs.

🐾 In captivity, gorillas have learned to communicate with human sign language.

# Fun Zone

**Gorillas eat plants and insects. These foods help them to grow up strong.**

This snack looks like gorilla food, but it is tasty and healthy for kids.

## Ants on a Stick

What You Need:

- Pieces of celery

- Raisins

- Peanut butter or cream cheese

What You Do:

Spread peanut butter or cream cheese on the celery pieces.

Put a line of raisins on top of the peanut butter or cream cheese so that they look like ants crawling along a stem.

Eat the celery "stem" and raisin "ants" like a hungry little gorilla.

# Wild Words

**Gorilla:** a large ape that lives in Africa

**Grunt:** a soft noise that sounds like "ooh-ooh"

**Silverback:** a big father gorilla that has silver hair on his back; the leader of a gorilla troop

**Troop:** a gorilla family; a troop usually has six to twelve members

**Rainforest:** a type of forest that has many trees and lots of rain

## Dig Deeper

WANT TO FIND OUT EVEN MORE ABOUT GORILLAS?

Check out the Ranger Rick website: www.RangerRick.com SEARCH: gorillas